Major One Octave | Majeur sur une octave*

♯ = Sharp / Dièse ♭ = Flat / Bémol ♮ = Natural / Bécarre

Ré Majeur
D Major

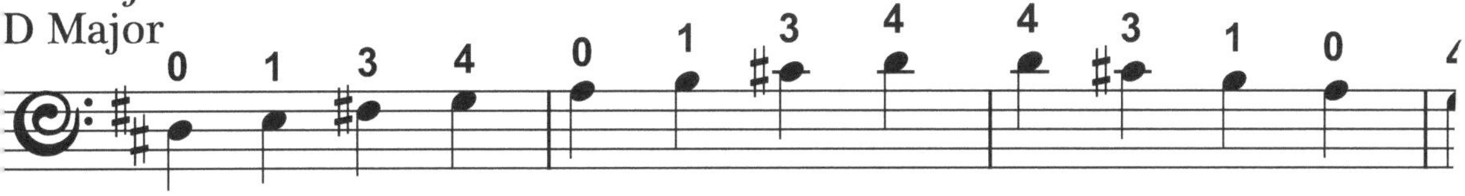

Sol Majeur
G Major

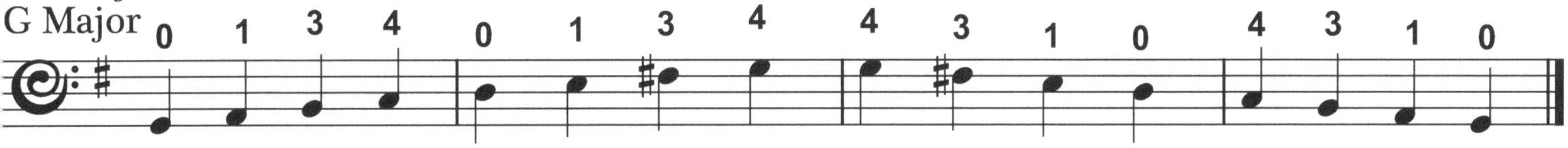

Do Majeur
C Major

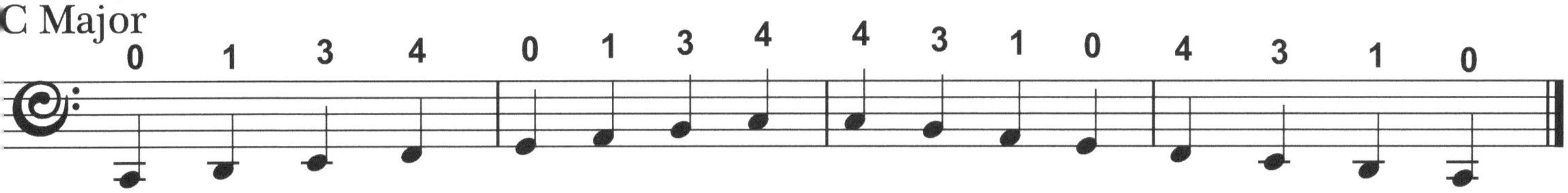

La Majeur
A Major

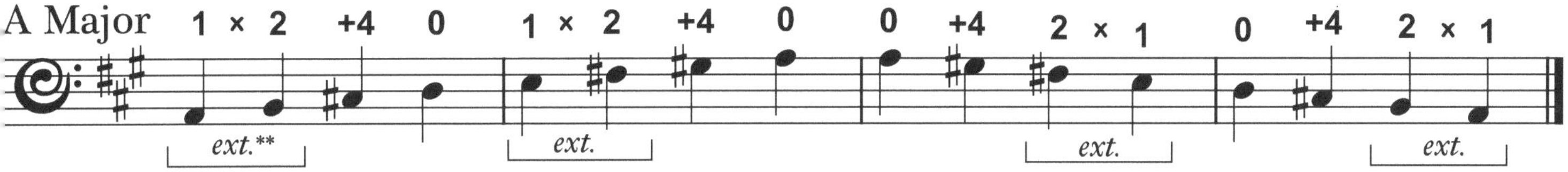

** *ext.* = extension : entre l'index et le majeur sur le manche | Between 1st & 2nd along the neck

Fa Majeur
F Major

Si ♭Majeur
B♭ Major

Mi ♭ Majeur
E♭ Major

*Séquence d'intervalles = ♩ - 1 - ♩ - 1 - ♩ - ½ - ♩ - 1 - ♩ - 1 - ♩ - 1 - ♩ - ½ - ♩

* Interval sequence = ♩ - W - ♩ - W - ♩ - h - ♩ - W - ♩ - W - ♩ - W - ♩ - h - ♩

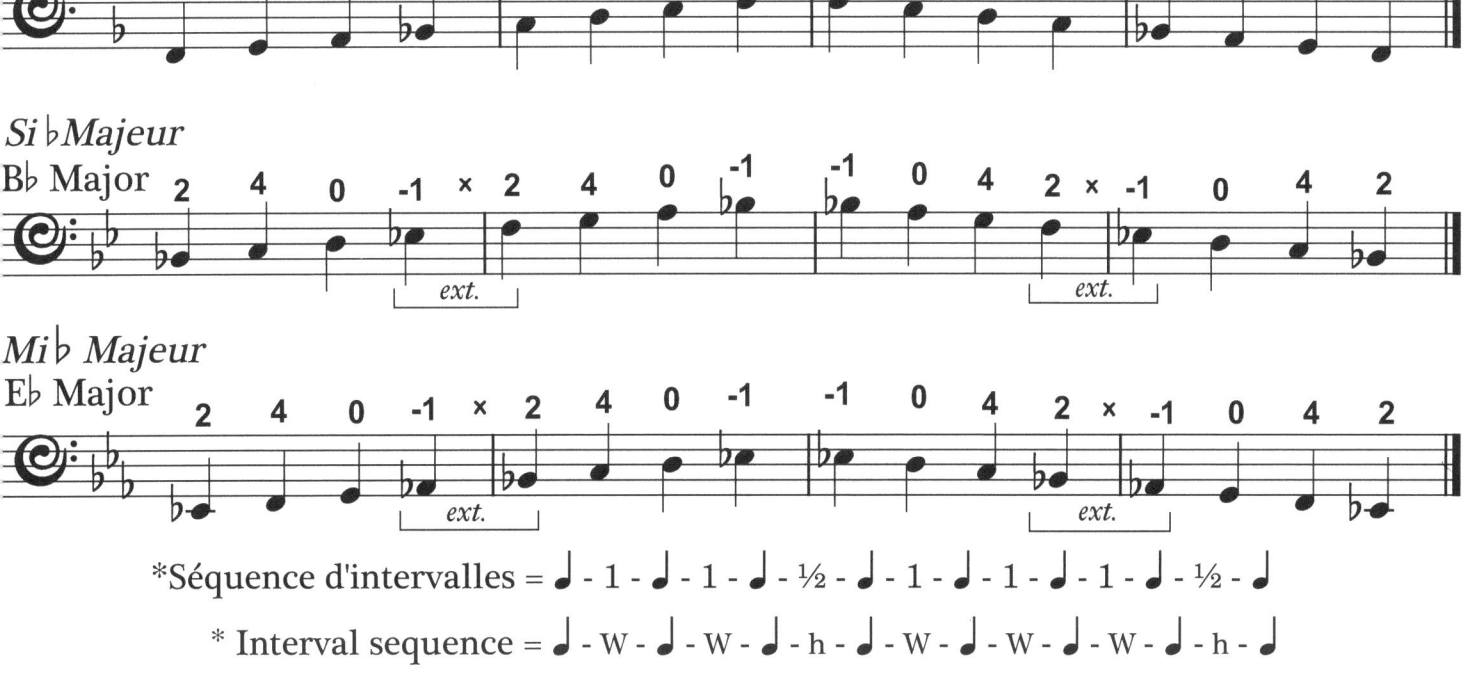

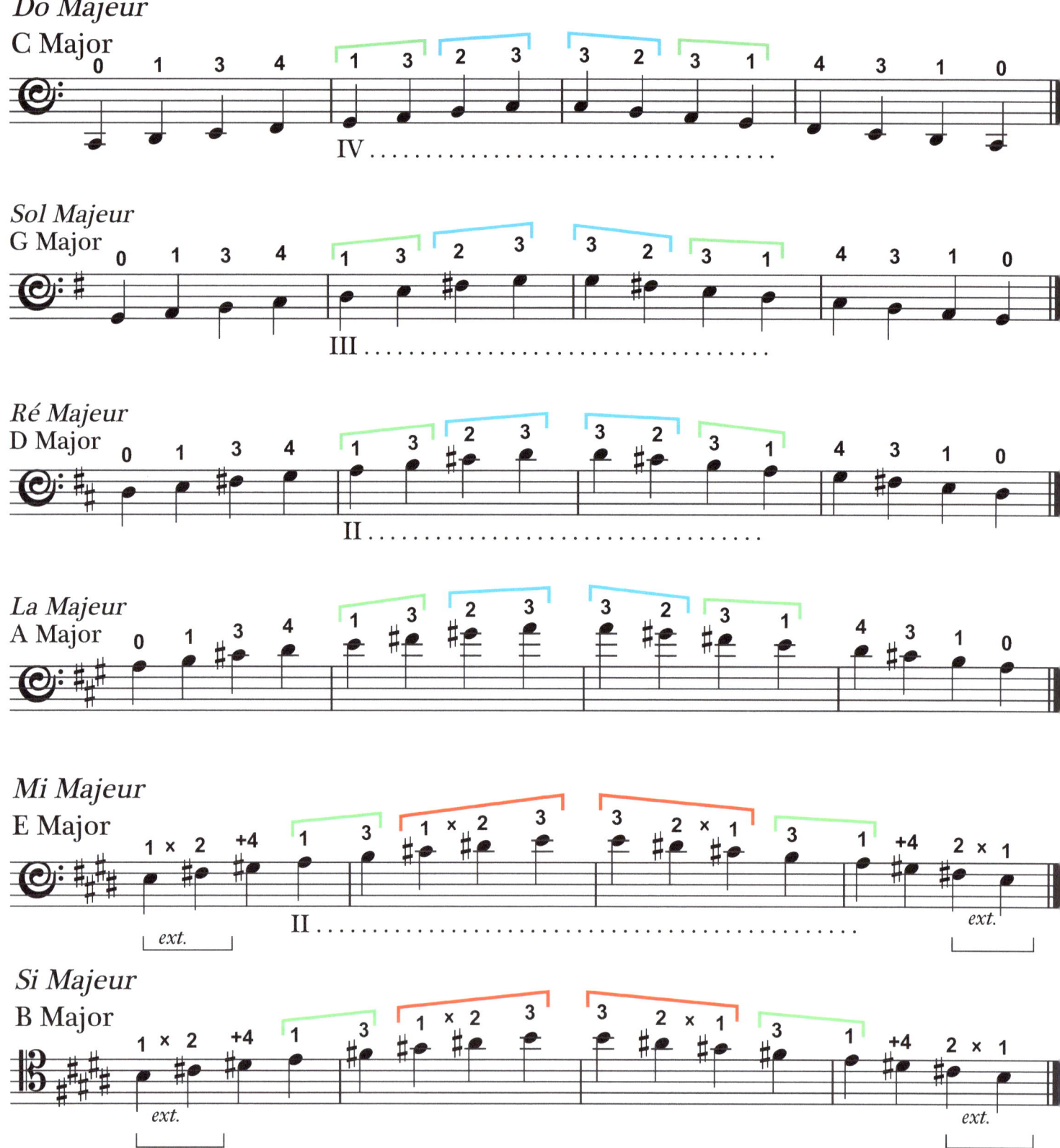

The Tenor Clef

Cellists use tenor clef to help read notes primarily on the A string from A3 up to E5, from 1st position to Thumb 1. Tenor clef helps us avoid reading excessive ledger lines.

Nous utilisons la clé d'ut pour lire plus facilement les notes situées principalement sur la corde de La, de la 1ère position jusqu'à la position du pouce.

Quick tip: In tenor clef, the open A sits in the middle of the stave (just like open D in bass clef), and the top line is now E4 - 1st finger in 4th position on the A string.

Petit conseil: En clé d'ut, le La à vide se trouve au milieu de la portée (comme le Ré à vide en clé de fa), et la ligne supérieure de la portée correspondun cle d'ut a la 1ère doigt en 4ème position sur la corde de La.

Our 3 Clefs | Nos 3 Clés

Bass clef - clé de *Fa*

Tenor clef - clé *d'Ut*

Treble clef - clé de *Sol*

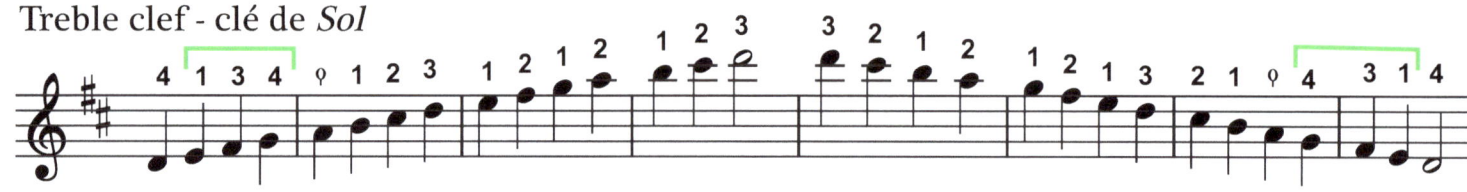

Major Arpeggios | Les Arpèges Majeurs

Scale degree - Degré d'échelle (I - III - V - I)   Fingerings - Doigtés (4 - 1 - 4 - 2)

Ré Majeur
D Major

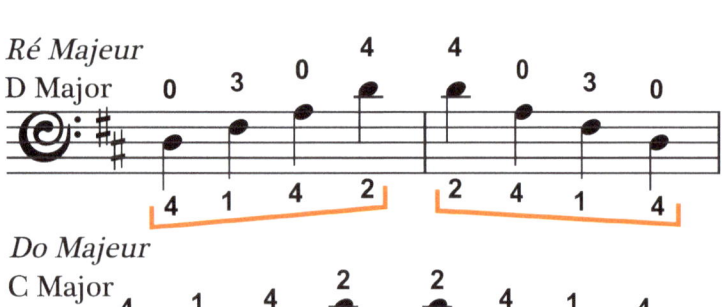

Do Majeur
C Major

Fa Majeur
F Major

Mi♭ Majeur
E♭ Major

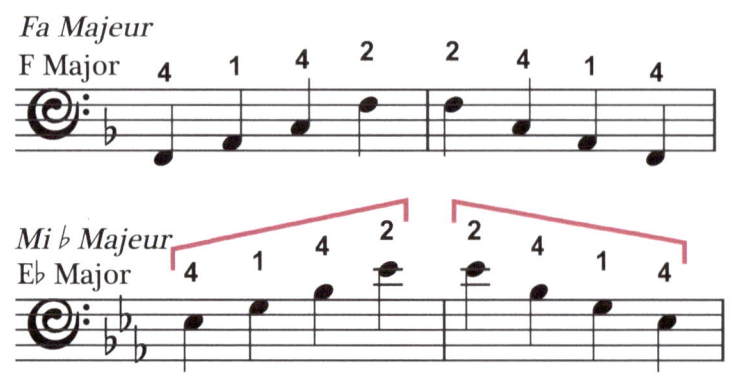

Sol Majeur
G Major

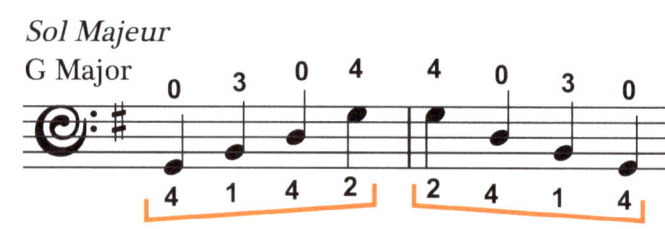

La Majeur
A Major

Si♭ Majeur
B♭ Major

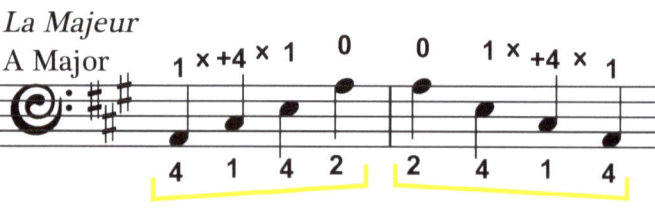

La♭ Majeur
A♭ Major

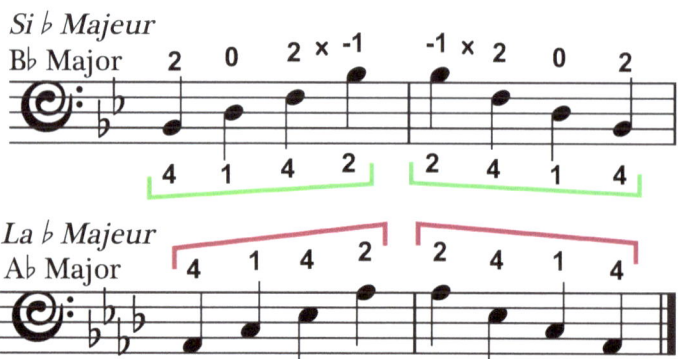

(4)

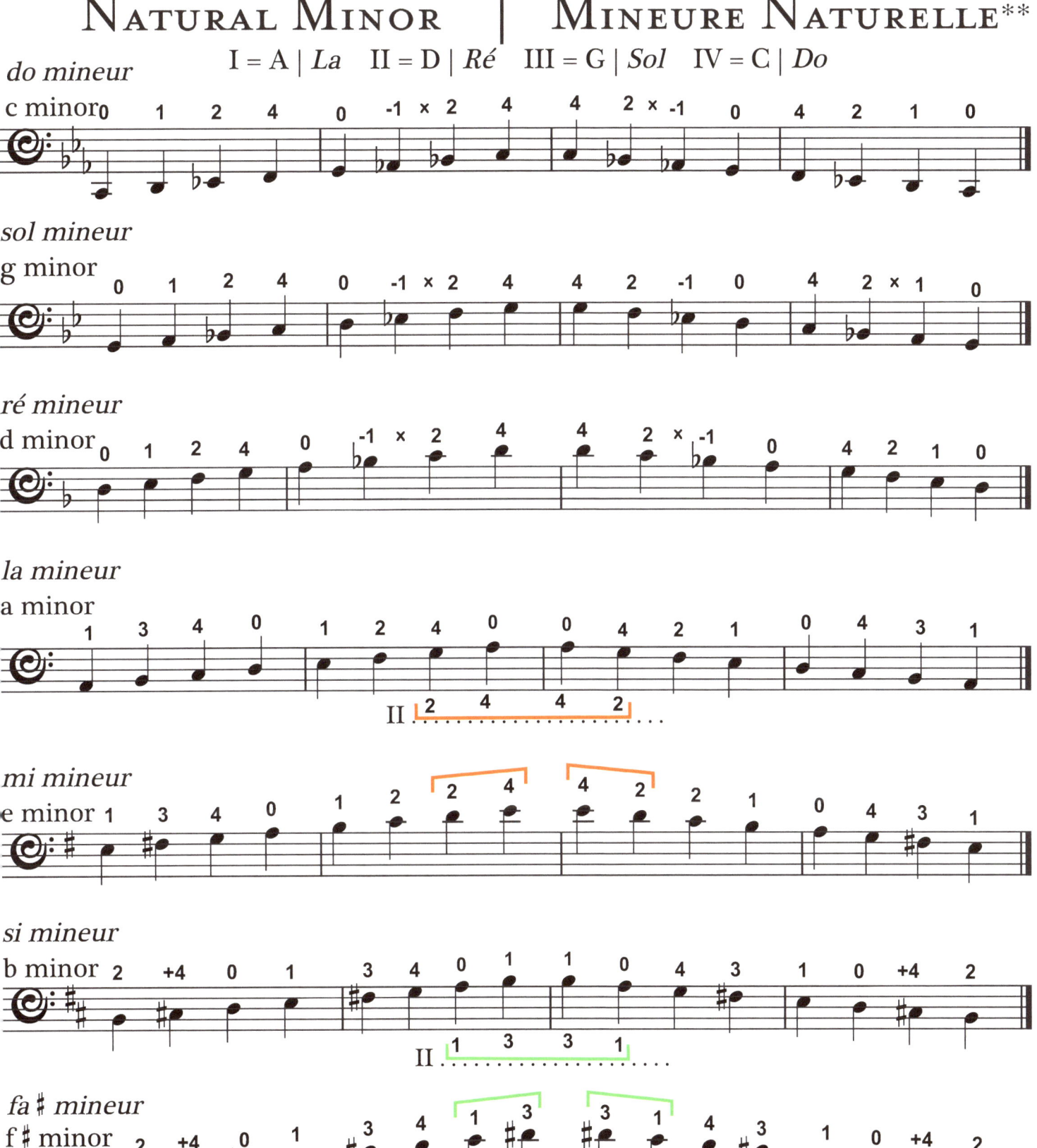

Octave on a String - Minor

Chaque mineur a son majeur | Every minor has its major

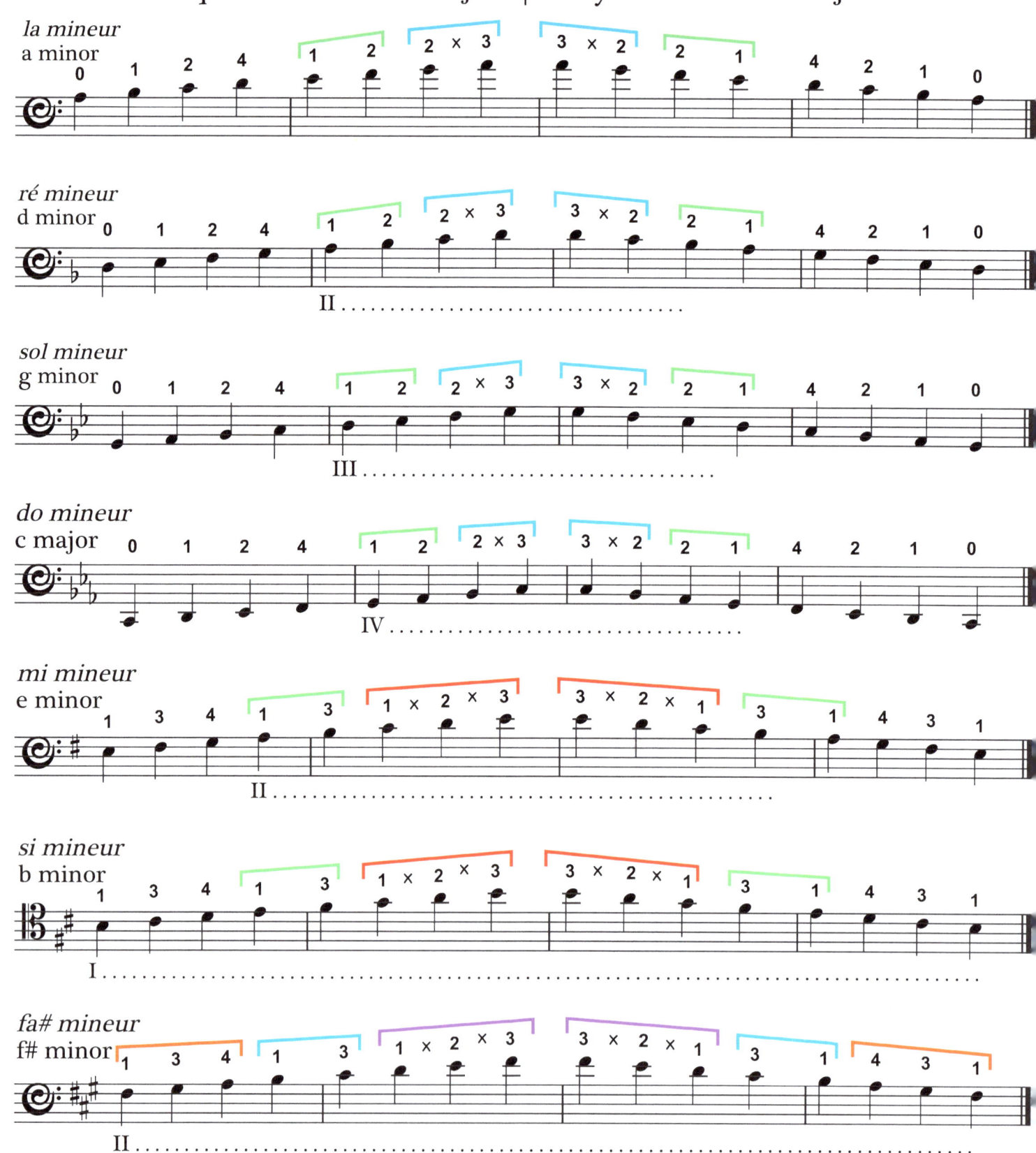

Music is for reference not for reading – Les partitions servent de repère, pas de lecture

Minor Arpeggios | Les arpèges mineurs

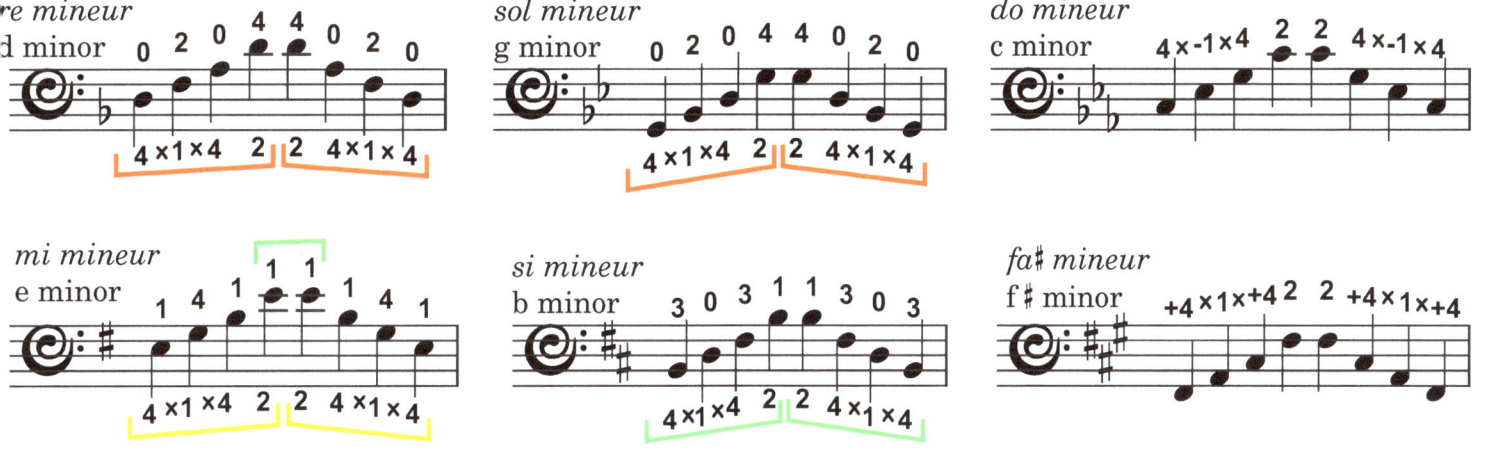

Harmonic Minor | Mineure Harmonique*

*raise the 7th note 1/2 tone ascending and descending

augmenter la 7ème note d'un demi ton me mourant et en descendant

Melodic Minor | Mineure Mélodique**

**** raise the 6th and 7th note 1/2 tone ascending,
revert back to the natural minor when desceding**

augmenter la 6ème et 7ème note d'un demi ton en montant,
et puis revenir à la mineure naturelle en descendant

Each minor scale reveals a unique color: natural for depth, harmonic for tension, and melodic for flow. Learning all three sharpens your ear, improves intonation, and gives you expressive control as a cellist. They're not just music theory : they're how emotion takes shape in sound.

Chaque gamme mineure révèle une couleur unique : naturelle pour la profondeur, harmonique pour la tension, et mélodique pour la fluidité. Les connaître toutes affine l'oreille, renforce la justesse et développe le contrôle expressif du violoncelliste. Ce ne sont pas que des notions théoriques musicales : c'est la manière dont l'émotion prend forme dans le son.

Major Two Octaves | Majeure à deux octaves

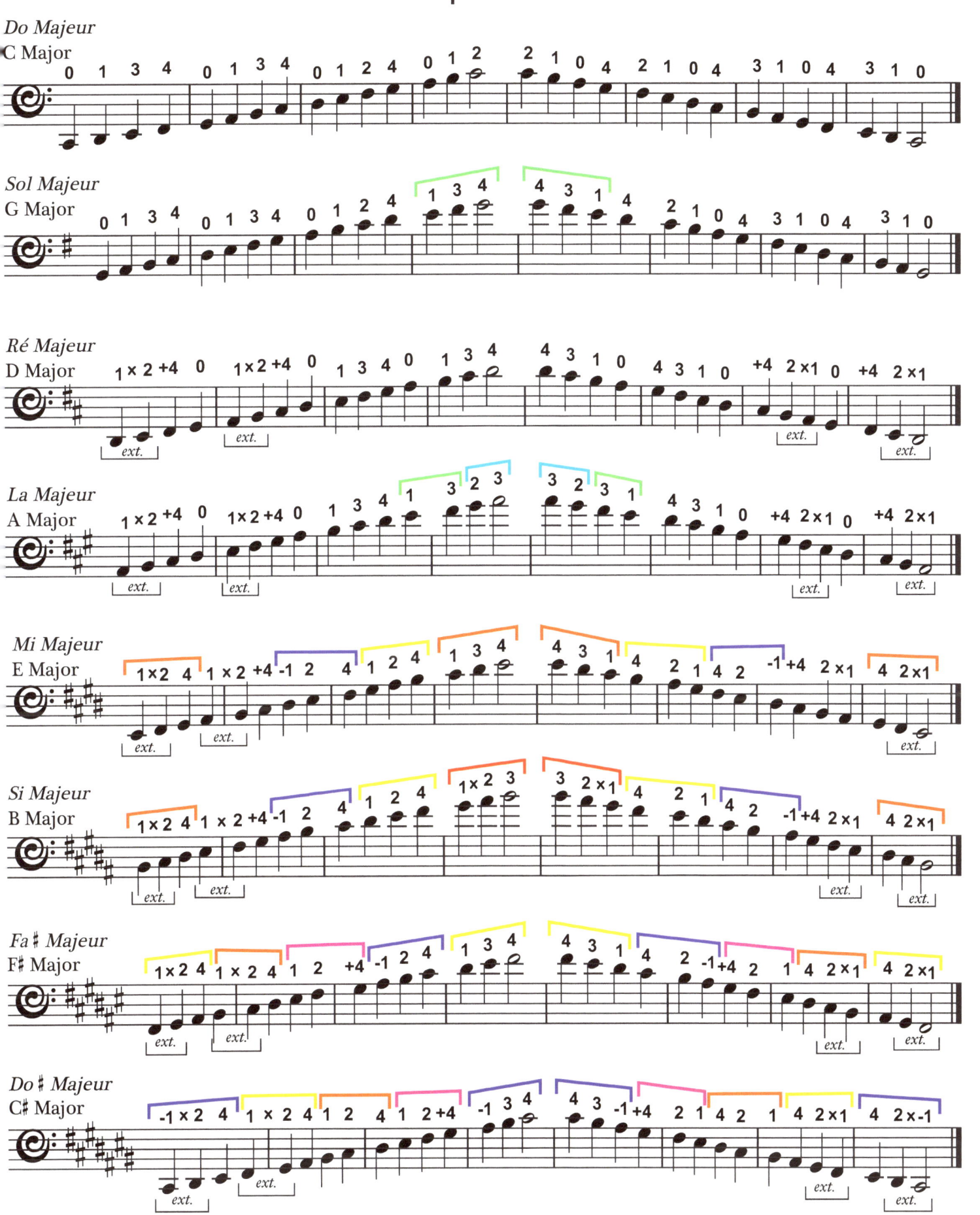

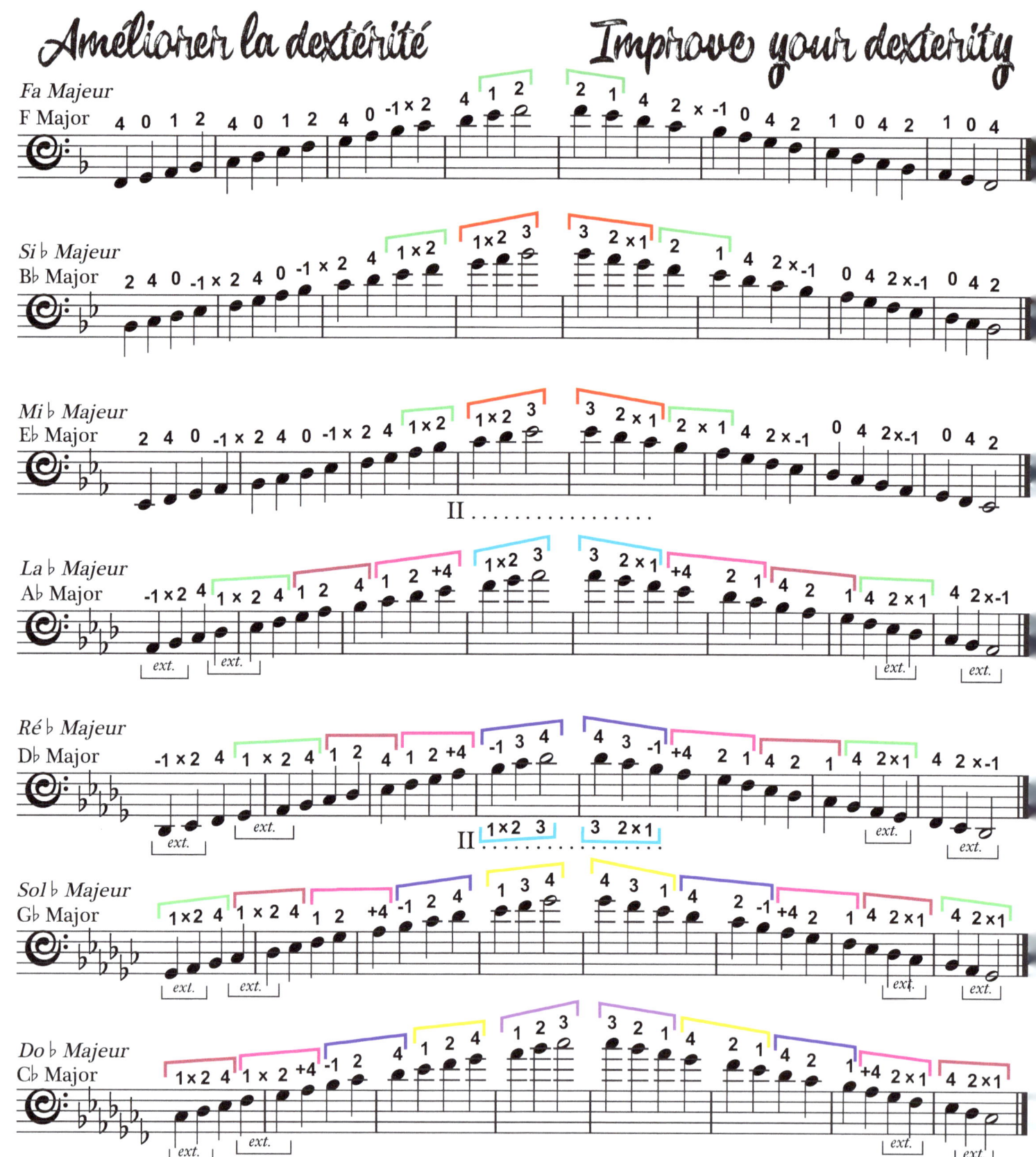

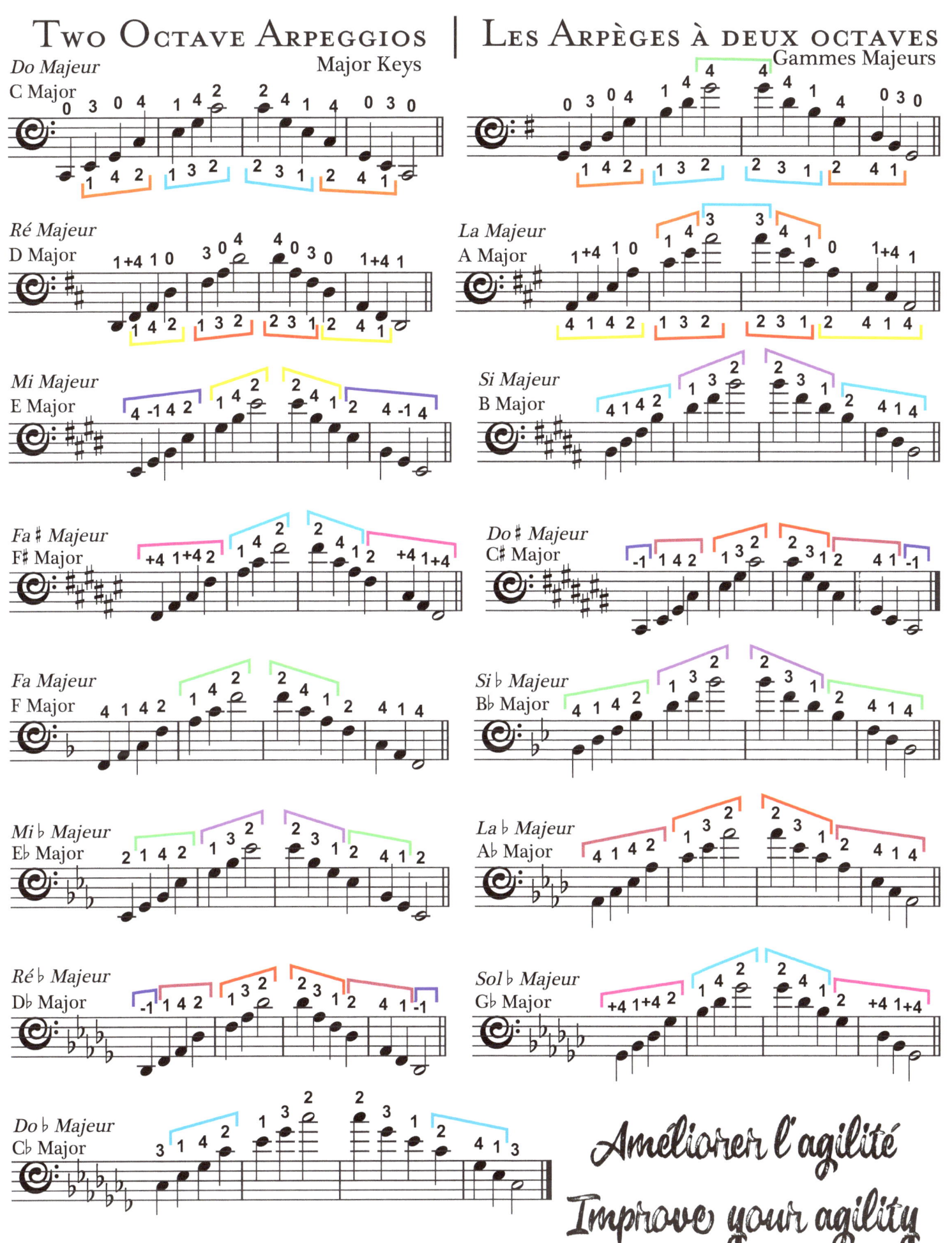

Minor Two Octaves | Mineure à deux octaves
Natural - Harmonic - Melodic   Naturelle - Harmonique - Mélodique

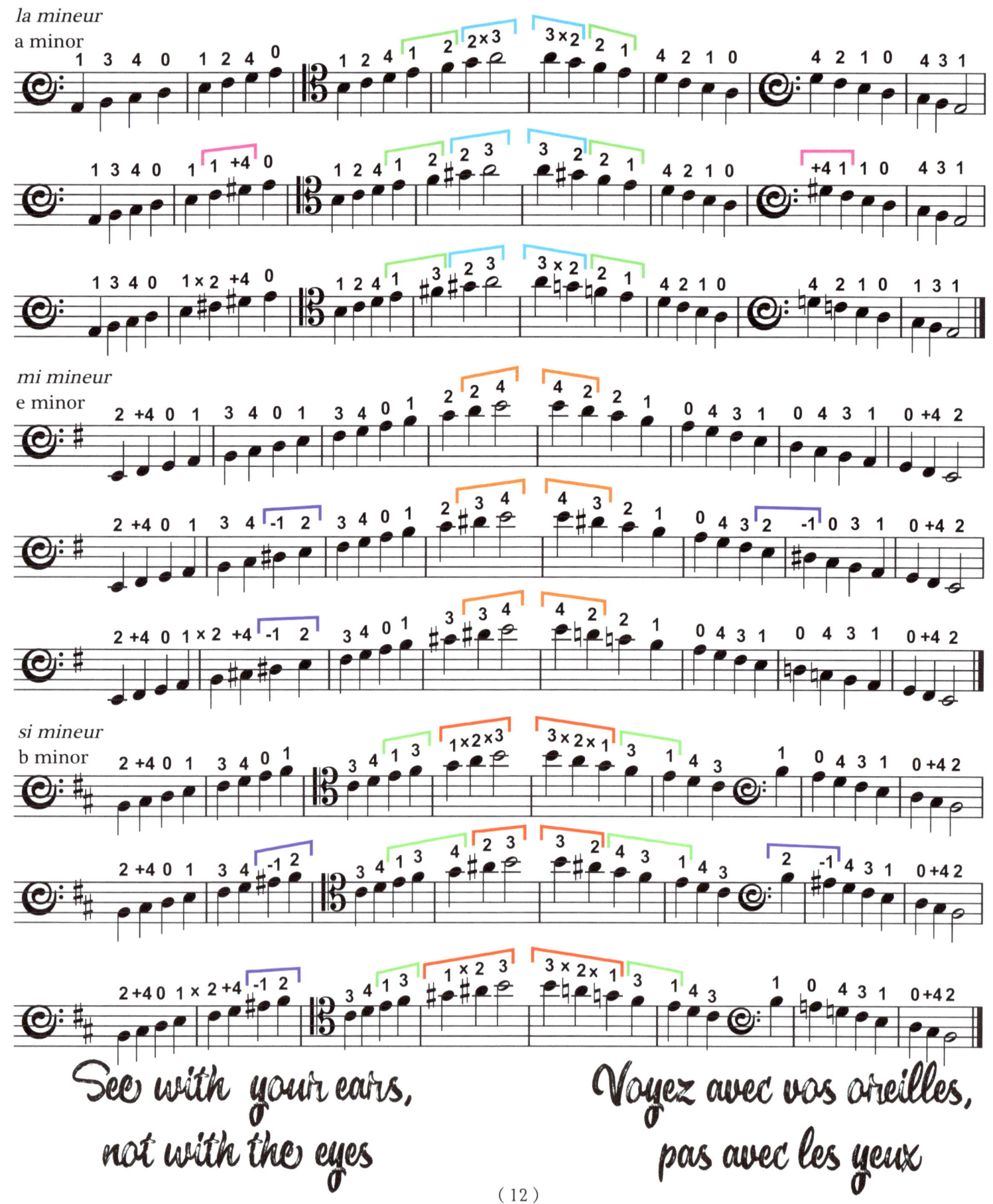

Il faut connaître la gamme naturelle mineure avant d'apprendre les variantes.

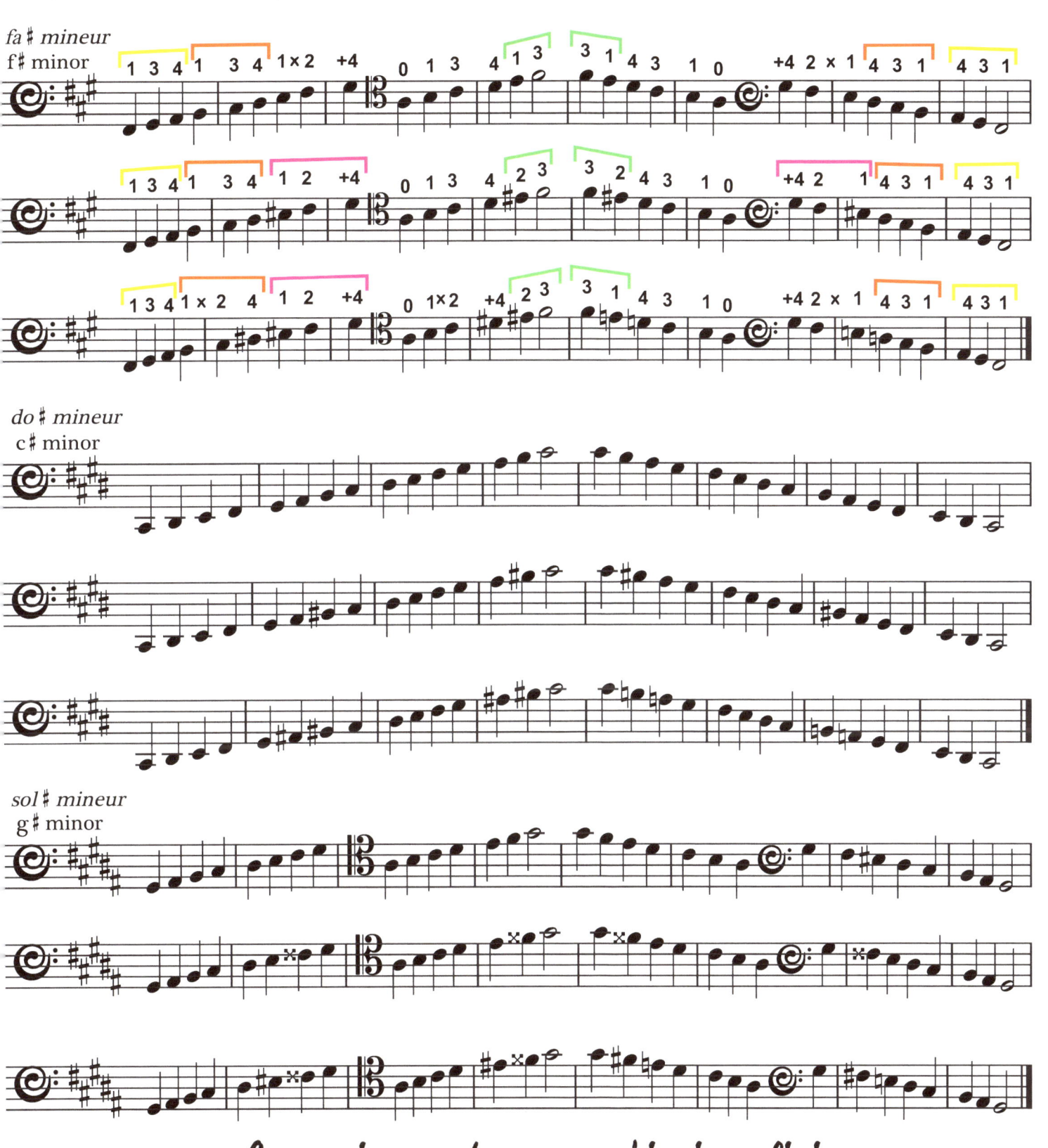

La musique est une combinaison finie
de sons et de silences qui est mesurée dans le temps.

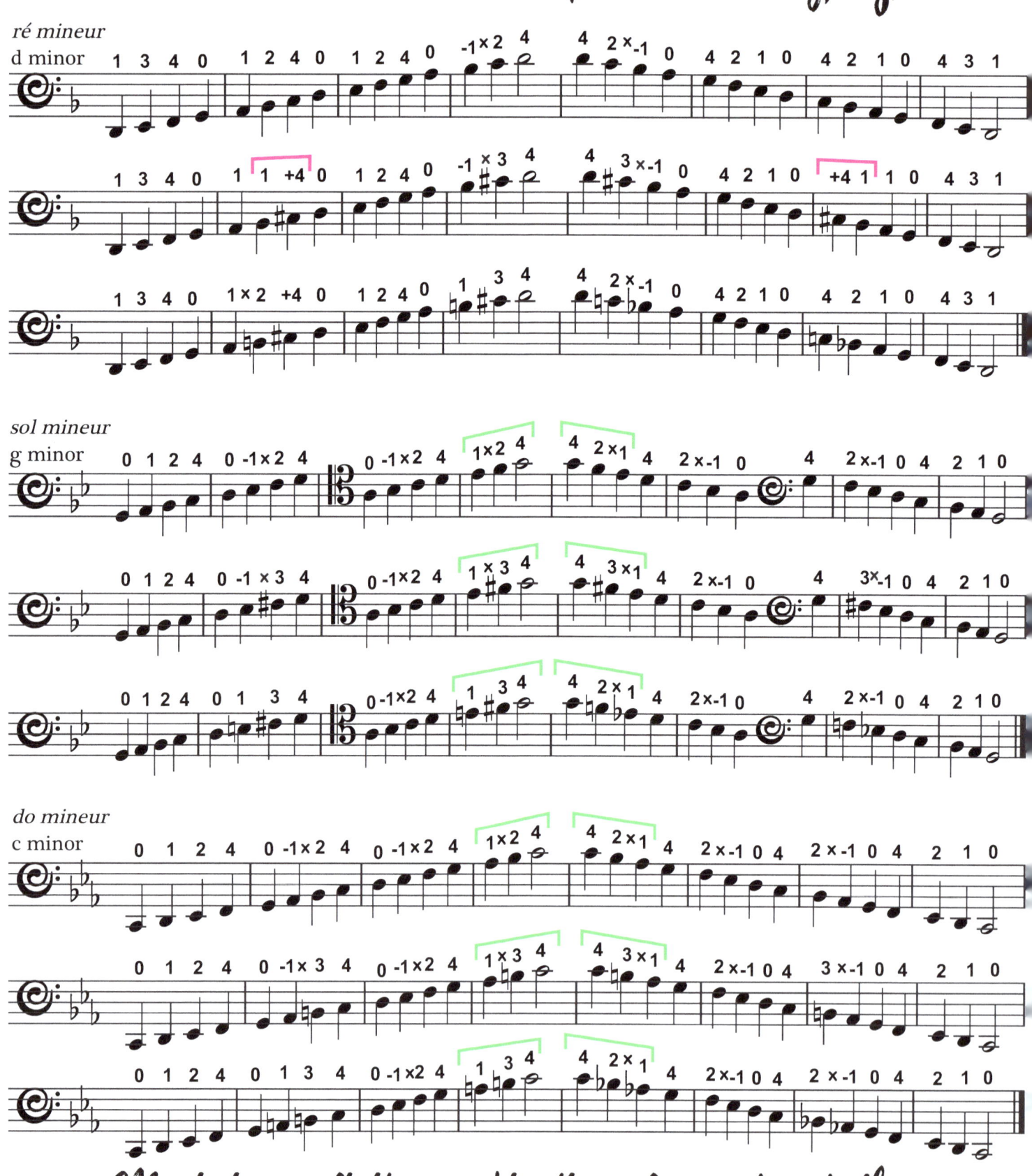

Nothing is difficult, only undiscovered   *Rien n'est difficile, juste inconnu*

fa mineur
f minor

si♭ mineur
b♭ minor

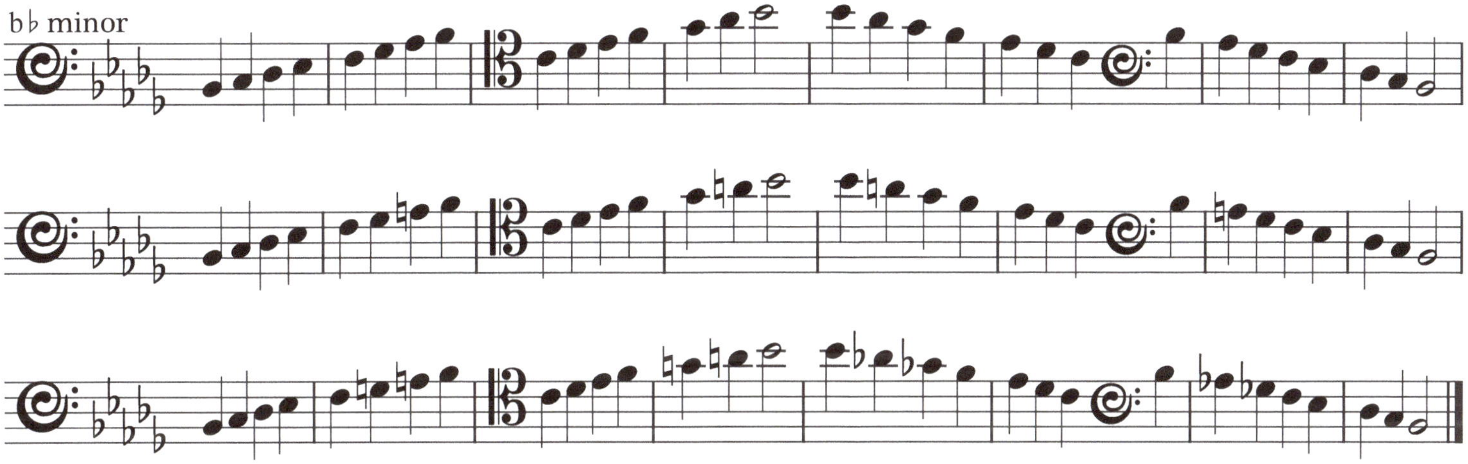

YOUR JOURNEY

STUDENT _____

TECHNICIAN _____

PLAYER _____

MUSICIAN _____

Cello is a world of opposites

VOTRE AVENTURE

ÉTUDIANT _____

TECHNICIEN _____

JOUEUR _____

MUSICIEN _____

Le violoncelle est un monde de contraires

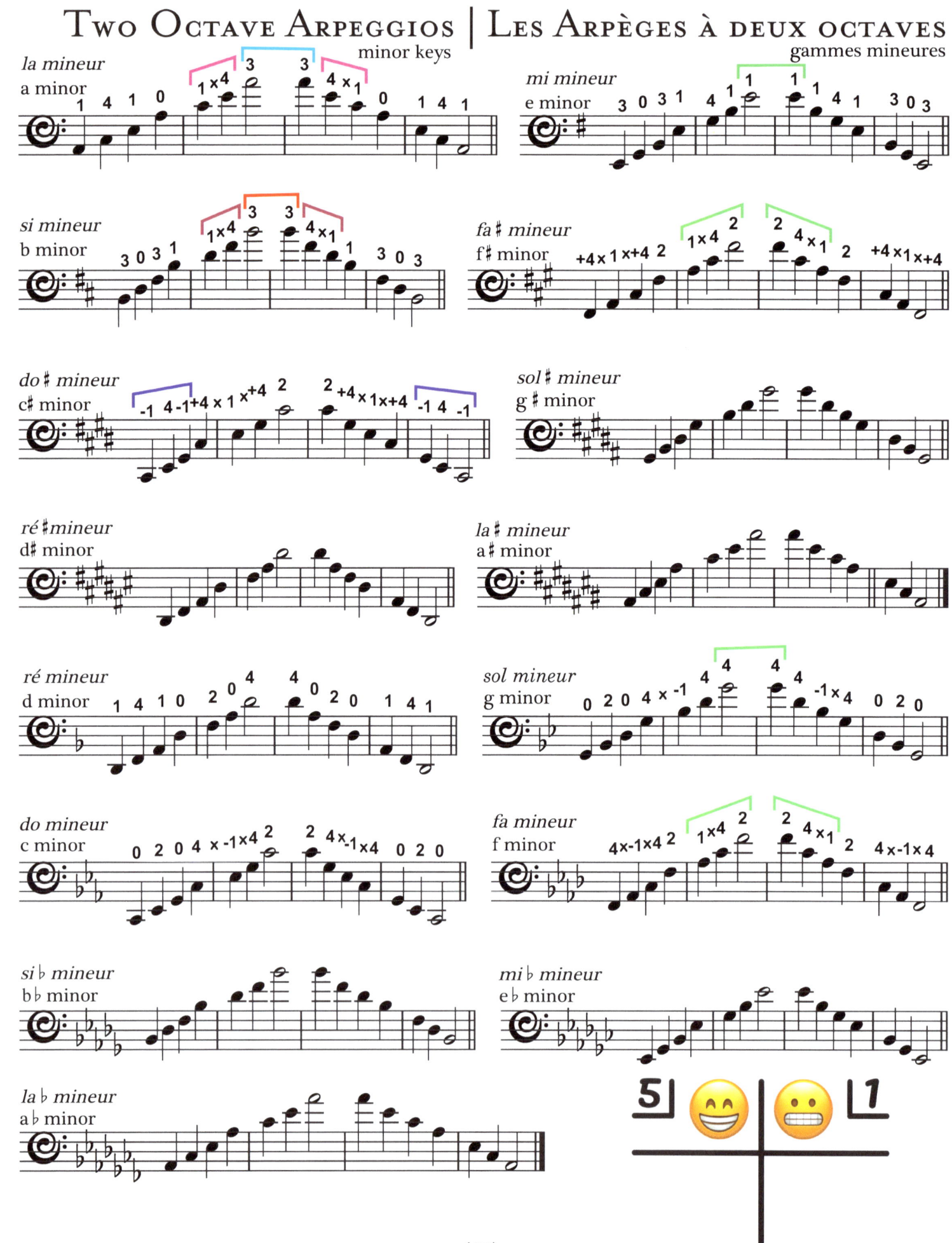

Pentatonic | Petatonique

♩ The *pentatonic* scale uses only five notes from all of the major or minor diatonic scales.

♩ It's easier to hear and play because there are no half steps, giving it an open, natural sound.

♩ Think of it as a bridge between arpeggios and scales - perfect for connecting patterns on the cello.

♪ Major Pentatonic I – II – III – V – VI   ⇨   in G (Sol) Major : G – A – B – D – E

♪ minor pentatonic i – iii – IV – V – ♭VII   ⇨   in g (sol) minor : G – B♭ – C – D – F

♩ La gamme *pentatonique* utilise cinq notes issues de n'importe quelle gamme majeure ou mineure.

♩ Elle est plus facile à entendre, car elle ne contient aucun demi-ton, ce qui lui donne un son ouvert.

♩ Considérez-la comme un pont entre les arpèges et les gammes, idéale pour relier les positions

G Major - Sol Majeur Diatonic**   G Major - Sol Majeur Pentatonic

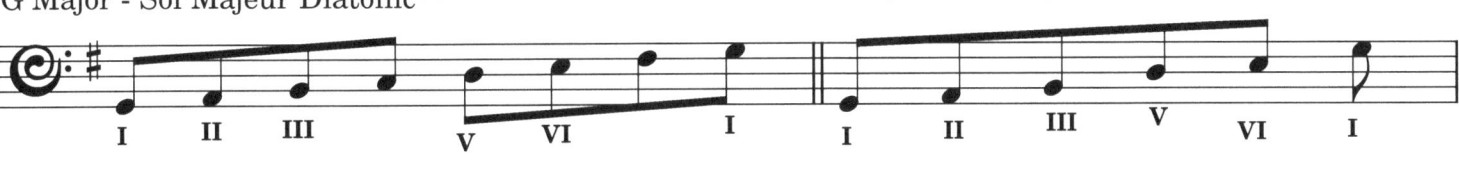

G Major - Sol Majeur Pentatonic

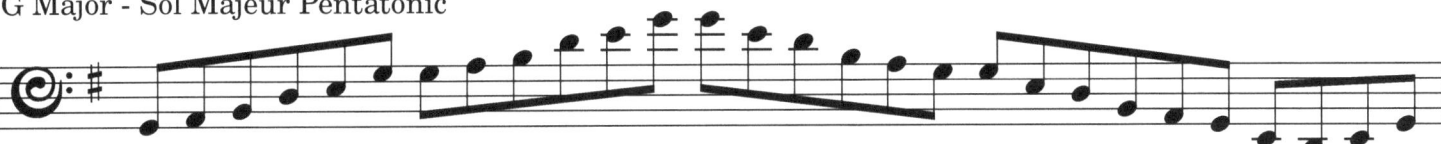

g minor - sol mineur diatonic   g minor - sol mineur pentatonic

g minor - sol mienur pentatonic 2 octaves

* Pentatonic Logic | Logique pentatonique**

First, learn your diatonic scales — 7 notes where you can clearly feel the half steps and whole steps.

Once you understand that pattern, remove the two half steps to form the pentatonic.

The goal is to learn it by ear and memory, not by reading.

Apprenez d'abord vos gammes diatoniques — sept notes avec leurs demi-tons et tons entiers.

Une fois le schéma compris, retirez les deux demi-tons pour former la pentatonique.

L'objectif est de l'apprendre à l'oreille et par cœur, sans partition.

Pentatonic Major (I - II - III - V - VI)

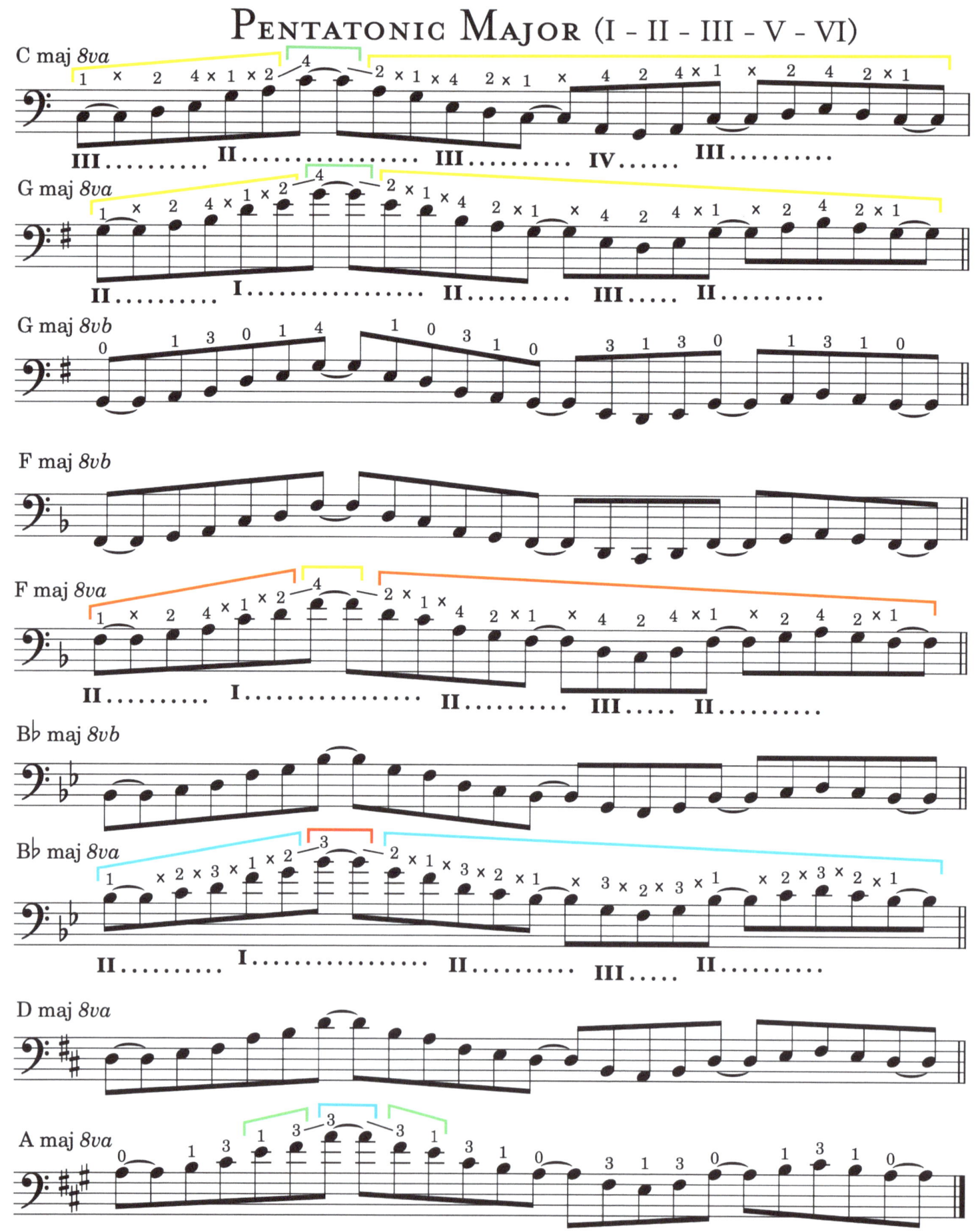

(17a)

Work / Labor

Arpeggios	Positions
Articulation	Prep
Bowing	Posture
Bow Control	Relax
Bow Hold	Rhythm
Breathe	Scales
Confidence	Shift
Discovery	Tempo
Dynamics	Theory
Fingerings	Timing
Intonation	Tone
Musicality	Tuning
LH technique	Warm Up

Your Priorities / Vos Priorités

_____   _____
_____   _____
_____   _____
_____   _____
_____   _____
_____   _____
_____   _____

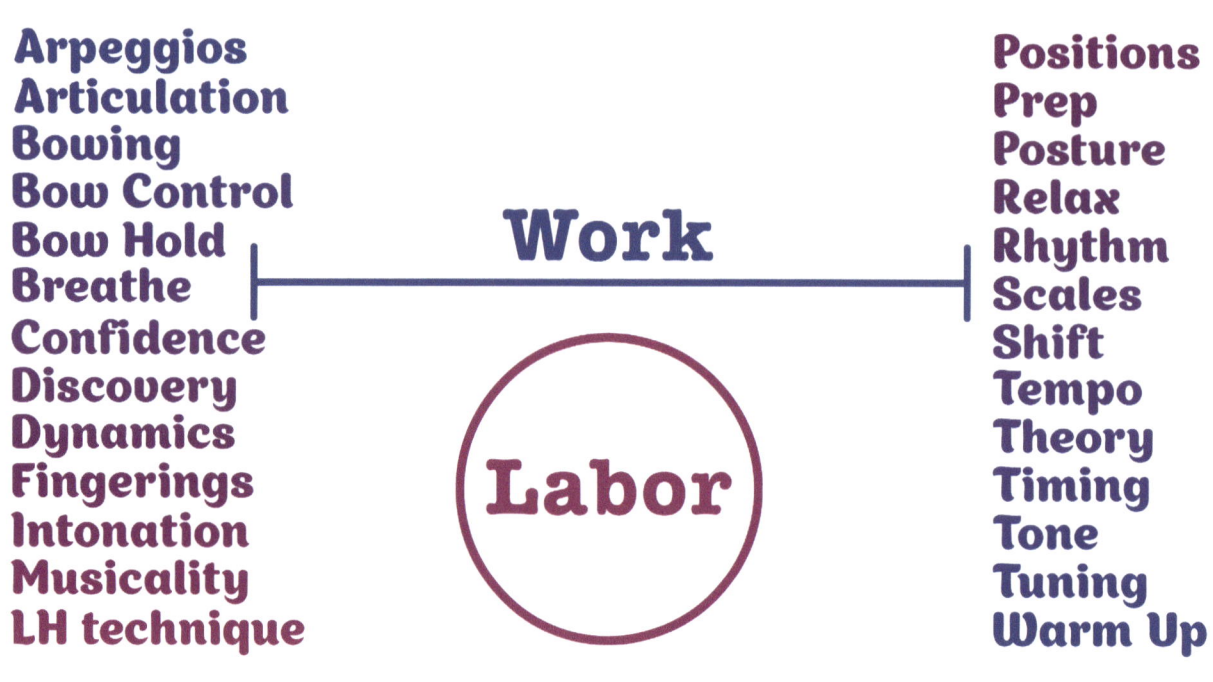

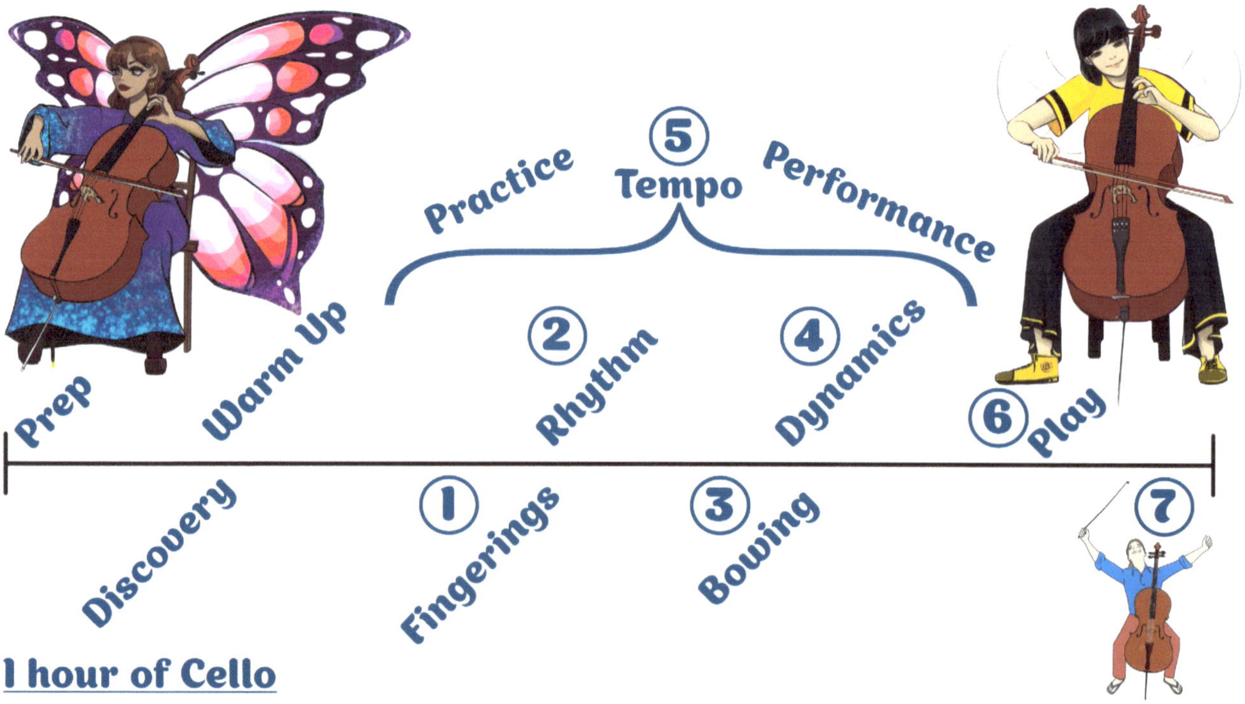

1 hour of Cello

Prep — Warm Up — Discovery — ① Fingerings — ② Rhythm — { Practice — ⑤ Tempo — Performance } — ③ Bowing — ④ Dynamics — ⑥ Play — ⑦

Third Octave | Troisième octave
(1 2) → (1 2) → (1 2 3)

Do Majeur
C Major

Sol Majeur
G Major

Ré Majeur
D Major

La Majeur
A Major

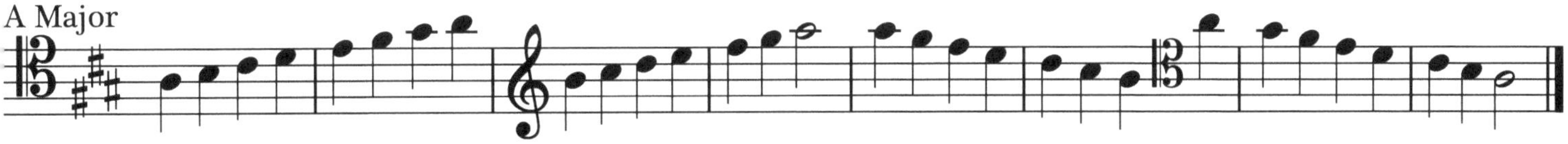

Mi Majeur
E Major

Fa Majeur
F Major

Si♭ Majeur
B♭ Major

Mi♭ Majeur
E♭ Major

La♭ Majeur
A♭ Major

Minor Melodic 3 Octaves | Mineur à Trois Octaves

la mineur
a minor

ré mineur
d minor

sol mineur
g minor

do mineur
c minor

fa mineur
f minor

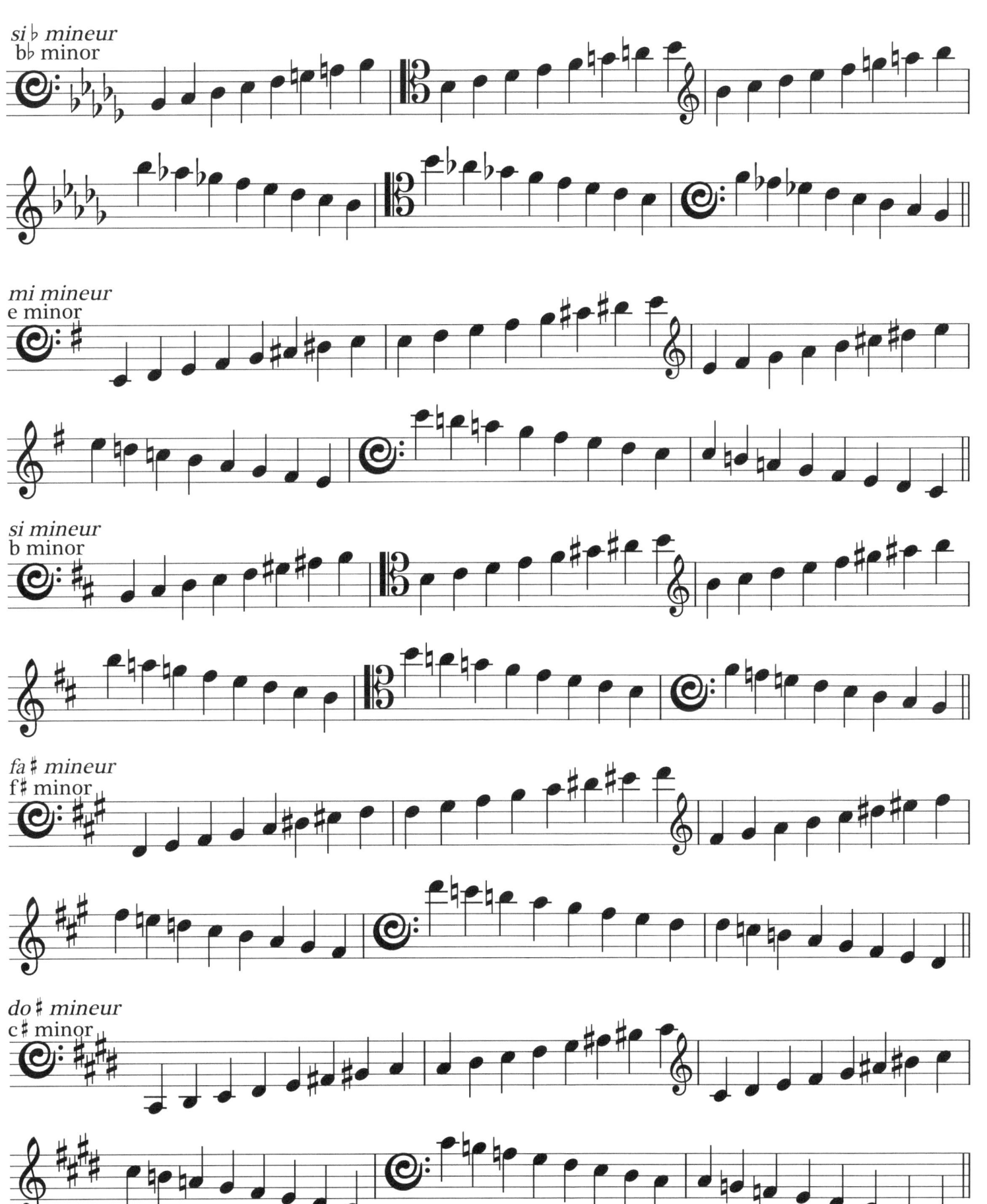

Thumb Position | Position du Pouce

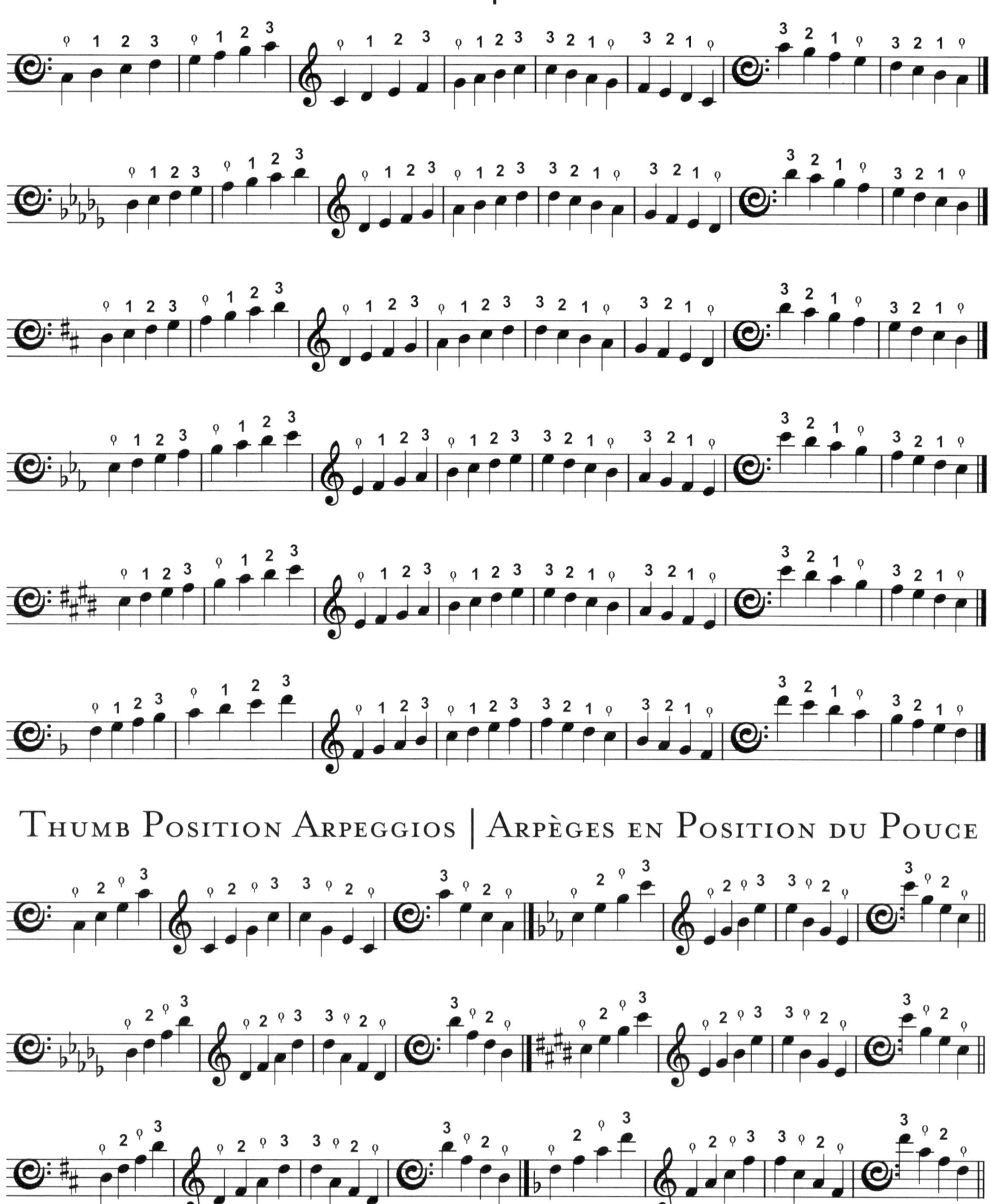

Thumb Position Arpeggios | Arpèges en Position du Pouce

Carl Flesch Arpeggios

☞ Drop a 5th with the same fingerings | Decendrez d'un 5ème avec les mêmes doigtés ☜

4 Octave Arpeggios | Arpèges à 4 Octaves

E♭ Major – Mi♭ Major

A♭ Major – La♭ Major

The Vocabulary of Cello

<u>Articulations</u> - tell the cellist how a note should be played

<u>Bowing</u> - the direction a cello bow moves ; *down* = pull to the right ; *up* = push to the left

<u>Arco</u> (Spanish : bow) - play with the bow

<u>Pizzicato</u> (pizz) (Italian : pinched) - pluck the string with the right hand index or middle finger

<u>Portato</u> (Italian : to carry) - slightly detached yet connected notes played in a single bow stroke

<u>Staccato</u> (Italian : detached) - shorten the note

<u>Spiccatto</u> - (Italian : to separate) play with the bow short and lightly, bouncing on string

<u>Tenuto</u> (Italian : held) - play the note as long as possible

<u>Détaché</u> (French : detached) - a brushed bowstroke, longer than spiccatto

<u>Martelé</u> (French : hammered) - fast, forceful bowstroke

<u>Sautillé</u> (French : skipped) - bow at the balance point, using the resiliency of the stick

<u>Sul tasto</u> - bow over the fingerboard

<u>Tremelo</u> - move the bow very fast & repeatedly on a single note, producing a trembling sound

<u>Vibrato</u> - subtle oscillation of the pitch with the left hand

<u>Dynamics</u> - the different volume changes of notes in music

<u>Sforzando</u> (Italian : forcing) - play the note with a sudden, strong emphasis and volume

<u>Con sordino</u> (Italian : with mute) - play with a mute

<u>Subito</u> (Italian : immediately) - a sudden change in dynamics

<u>Crescendo</u> (Italian : swelling) - increasing the music's volume

<u>Diminuendo</u> (Italian : decreasing) lowering of the music's volume

<u>Legato</u> (Italian : tied together) - play notes smoothly and connected, in one bow stroke

<u>Ritardando</u> - Slow down the trempo gradually

<u>Rubato</u> - temporary fluctuation of the tempo to allow for expression

<u>Meno mosso</u> - less movement or emotions

<u>Simile</u> - play the following notes or measures in the same manner

<u>D.C. al Fine</u> - return to the beginning, then finish where indicated Fine

<u>D.C. a la Coda</u> - return to the beginning, play until the Coda sign ⊕ , then finish the Coda section

From 5th position upwards, extensions are possible between ANY fingers, because the size of the intervals reduce the closer you play to the bridge

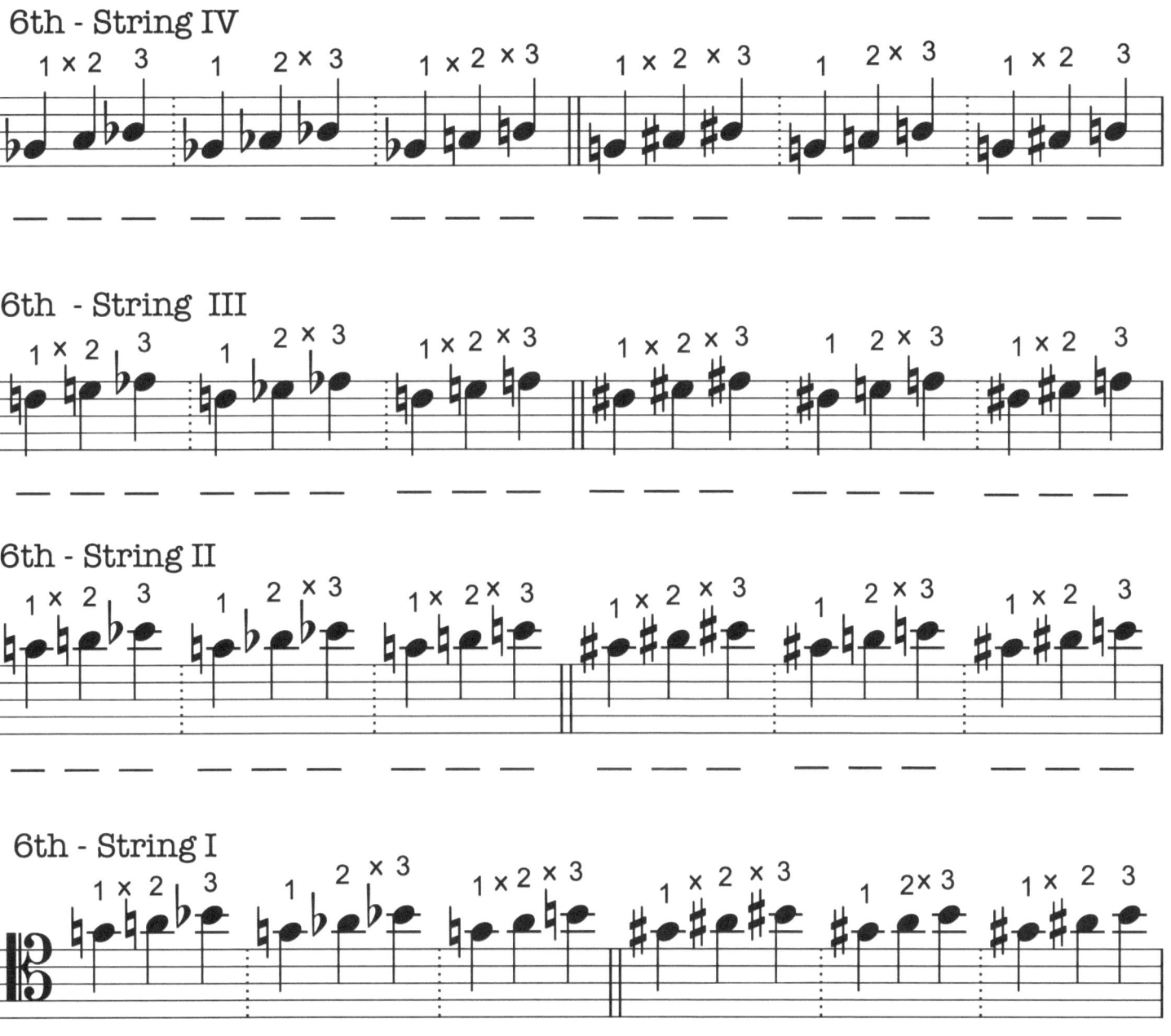

Left Hand Tip: Instead of pressing the string down to the fingerboard, pull it leftward by curling your fingertips and "hooking" the inside of the string. This can help prevent discomfort in awkward positions.

Vocabulaire du Violoncelle

Articulation - la longueur et la qualité de notes

Coup d'archet - la direction horizontale de l'archet : en tirant et en poussant

Arco - jouer avec l'archet

Pizzicato - Pincer avec les doigts de la main droite sur la moitié inférieure de la touche

Portato - Notes légèrement détachées mais liées dans un même coup d'archet.

Staccato - Jouer deux notes détachées et courtes dans un seul coup d'archet, sans soulever l'archet de la corde

Spiccato - Jouer notes rapides, coup d'archet léger et rebondissant

Tenuto - Note tenue, qu'on tient la longueur de la note en entier

Détaché - Jouer une note par archet. Jouer comme ça vient

Martelé - Coup d'archet vite et fort, court qui reste collé à la corde, notamment dans la moitié supérieure de l'archet.

Sautillé - Coup d'archet vite au point d'équilibre de la baguette, en se servant de la résistance de la baguette.

Sul tasto - On joue avec l'archet à niveau de la touche

Tremolo - Trembler: on joue des notes très vite et serrées dans une petite partie de l'archet

Vibrato - Vibrer avec la main gauche.

Nuances - Les différents volumes sonores

Sforzando - Jouer le début d'une note avec un effort soudain

Con sourdine - Avec sourdine   Subito - changement soudain de nuance

Crescendo - Augmenter le volume sonore   Diminuendo - Diminuer le volume sonore

Legato - Groupe de notes liées et jouées dans le même coup d'archet

Ritardando - Ralentir progressivement le mouvement et le tempo

Rubato - Fluctuation du tempo pour renforcer l'expression

Meno mosso - Changement de mouvement au plus lent

Simile - Faire les notes ou mesures suivantes de la même façon

D.C. al Fine - Rejouer au début jusqu'à la fin (fine)

D.C. a la Coda - rejouer au début jusqu'au signe ⊕ pour ensuite continuer à la coda

Notes

This book is the result of over twenty years of teaching, adapting, and reimagining how we learn the cello. Each new student brings new questions, new insights, and helps refine this method. Learning never stops — neither for the student, nor for the teacher. All of my scores available online use my color-coded bracket system, designed to make position work clear and intuitive. You can find these and more at www.CelloCoach.com (QR code below).

Ce livre est le fruit de plus de 20 ans d'enseignement, d'adaptation et de réinvention de l'apprentissage du violoncelle. Chaque élève apporte des questions, des idées et contribue à faire évoluer cette méthode. L'apprentissage ne s'arrête jamais — ni pour l'élève, ni pour le professeur. Toutes mes partitions disponibles en ligne utilisent mon système de crochets colorés, conçu pour rendre le travail des positions clair et intuitif. Vous pouvez les retrouver sur www.CelloCoach.com (QR code ci-dessous)

— Jonathan Humphries

Créateur de The CelloCoach Approach

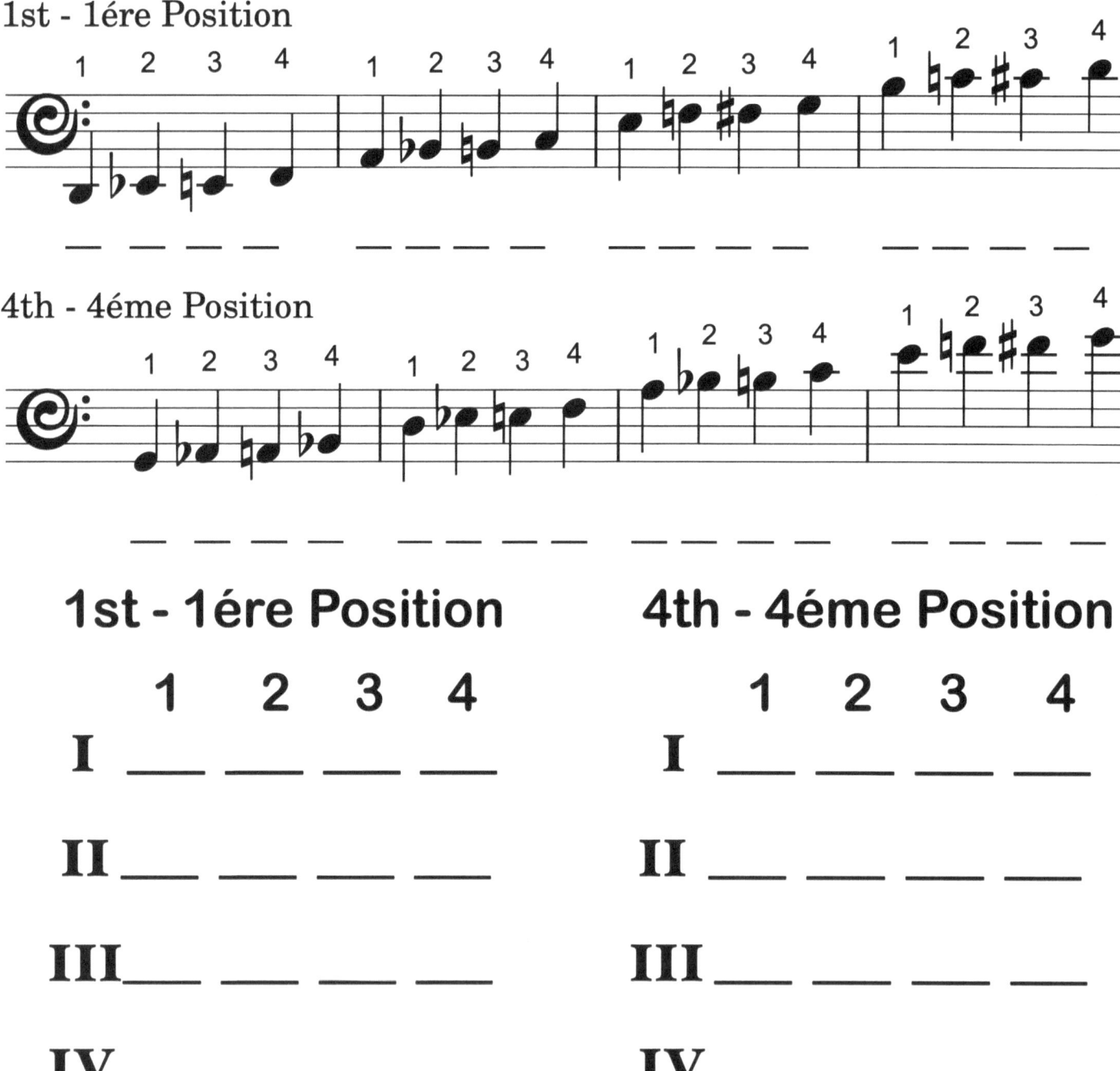

2nd & 3rd Positions

On the cello, lower notes are found closer to the scroll, while higher notes are played nearer the bridge. Cellists describe hand positions by pitch, not by physical direction. So even though your hand moves upward toward the scroll, the sound actually goes downward in pitch.

In lower positions, the fingers are spread farther apart, and the hand can't yet stretch evenly. For this reason, we divide positions into "lower" and "upper", depending on whether the index finger sits on the lower or higher of two possible notes.

By the time we reach 4th position, the notes are much closer spaced. The hand shape changes, and it becomes possible to extend comfortably between any fingers. From that point forward, there's no need to talk about "lower" or "upper" — just the position itself.

Half & 5th 6th 7th Positions

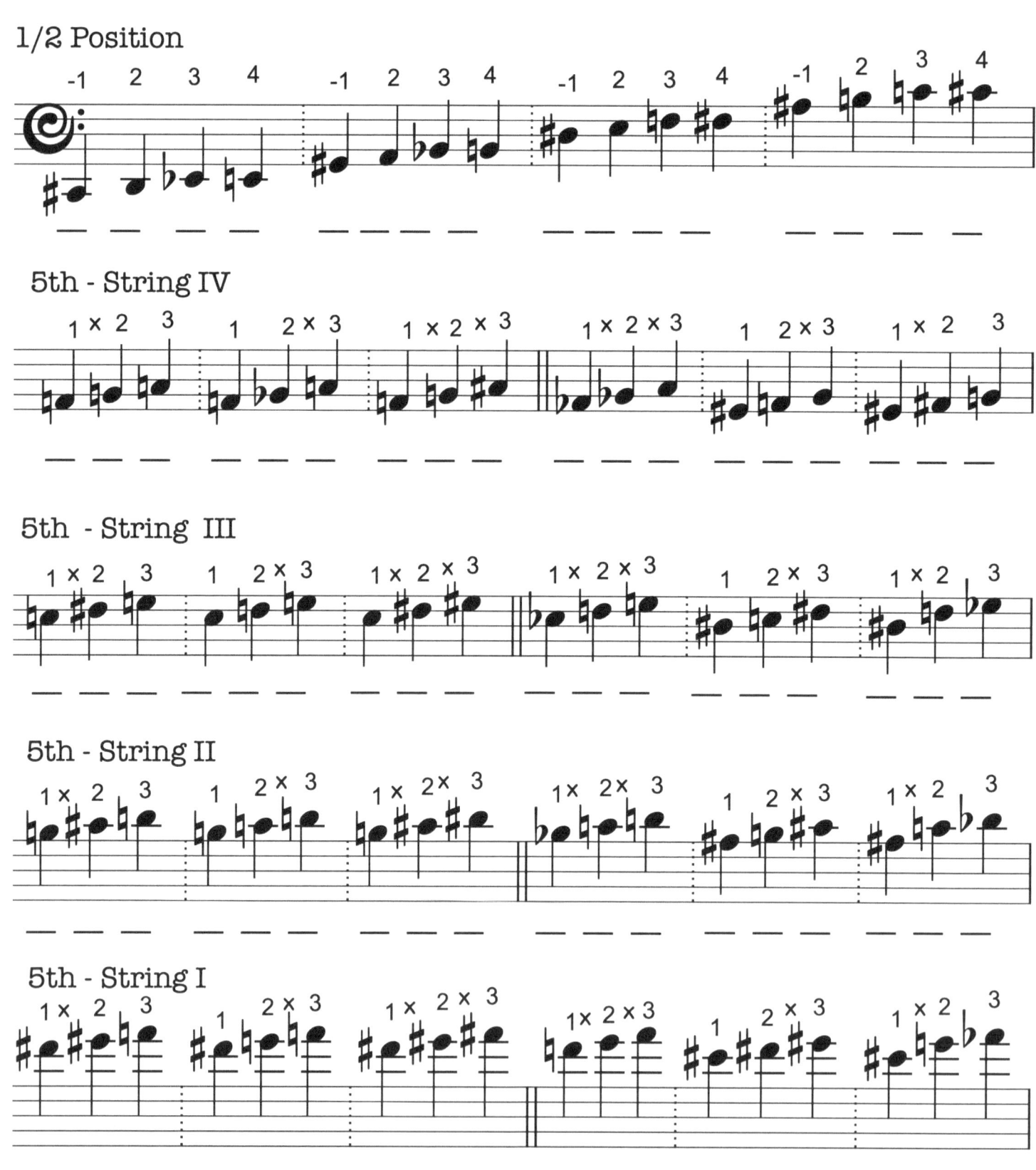

Appendix

7th - String III

7th - String II

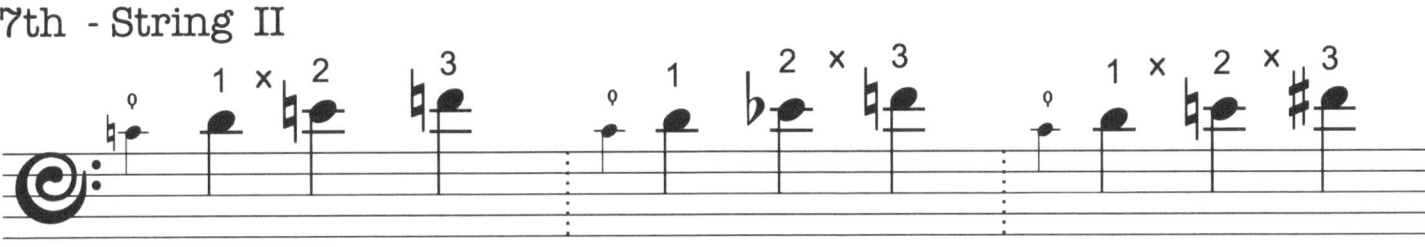

7th - String I

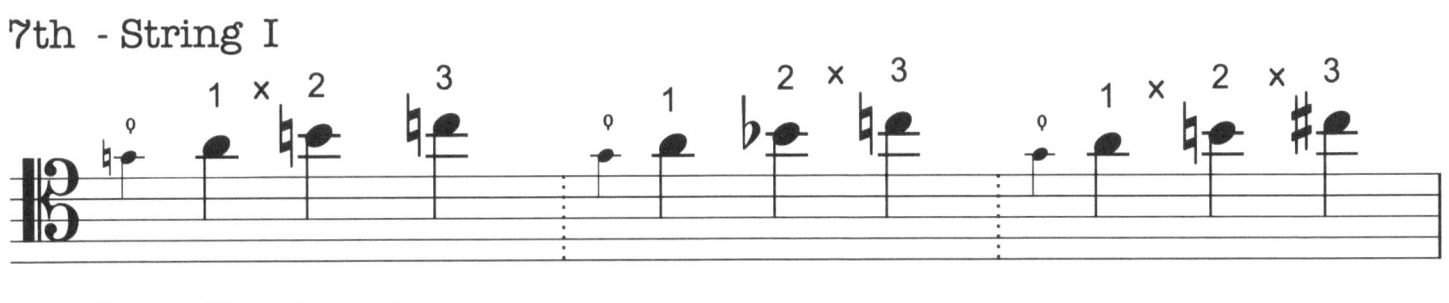

IMPORTANT : Keep your thumb flat across 2 strings, a whole tone below the index finger to maintain a proper "major" left hand thumb position

Notes : _____
_____
_____
_____
_____
_____
_____
_____
_____

CelloCoach Position Colour Guide (sRGB)

Position	Colour	Hex
Half		= 5F00DB
Lower 2nd		= F200C5
Upper 2nd		= E86C00
Lower 3rd		= C30665
Upper 3rd		= FFDD00
4th		= 0BFF8D
5th		= 00B2FF
6th		= FF4900
7th		= C46AFF

Scan this QR code to access The New Scale Book playlist

https://tinyurl.com/4p8t2dak

"Si le violoncelle n'était pas susceptible d'être doigté régulièrement, ce serait un instrument médiocre, mais ce n'est pas là le rang qu'il tient de nos jours parmi les instruments." — Jean-Louis Duport

The New Scale Book © 2013, 2018, 2020, 2023, 2025 by Jonathan Humphries

ALL RIGHTS RESERVED

No part of this publication may be reproduced, stored in a retrieval system or transmitted, in any form or by any means—electronic, mechanical, photocopying, recording or otherwise—without prior written permission, except for the inclusion of brief quotations in a review.

For more information contact : jh@jonathanhumphries.com | Tutorials : Youtube.com/TheCelloCoach

978-0-9859040-4-3 - Print Book   978-0-9859040-5-0 - eBook

www.ingramcontent.com/pod-product-compliance
Lightning Source LLC
Chambersburg PA
CBHW041527220426
43670CB00002B/48